#DearFutureWife

(365 Love Notes & Affirmations To My Future Love)

Ramel Werner

INTRODUCTION

God proves to be good to the man who passionately waits, to the woman who diligently seeks. It's a good thing to quietly hope for help from God. It's a good thing when you're young to stick it out through the hard times. When life is heavy and hard to take, go off by yourself. Enter the silence. Bow in prayer. Don't ask questions: Wait for hope to appear. - Lamentations 3:25-29 MSG

I wrote this book because when I write, it's easier to bare my soul. Sometimes if I have to speak it, it hides quietly behind my eyes waiting for you to see.

I don't expect to change the world in a big way, it's too old, too big, too overwhelming, but as an artist I must paint an accurate picture of what I want to convey given the right circumstances, the right person, and the right time.

Remember, you have the responsibility to protect and guide your heart. Don't give up and don't get discourage. Resolve to lead your heart and to make it through to the end of your search for a future soul mate. Learning to truly love is one of the most important things you will ever do. May God bless you as you begin to write or re-write your future mate.

CONTENTS

ACKNOWLEDGMENTS

I cannot express enough thanks to my family for their continued support and encouragement: Mom (Linda Walker) for always believing that there was better for me out there and to never give up on my dreams, Dad (Karl Werner) You're my hero man. To take such a path that you did and make it into what you are today... I thank you for my visuals of life lessons 101; My sister Cocoa (Khalia Ross) I wanted so much to give you a better road map on life while all the time your existence was truly all I needed to understand and respect that there are no instructions to being there for one another. You show me every day how to be the brother you needed all along.

Charlene, we met at a time where we both lost someone near and dear to our hearts. The connection between you and I was instantaneous. I still can't believe God saw fit to bless us with one of his children (Ryann). I couldn't asked for a better mother to our child. Thank you for being there with me through my latest milestones. You've sacrificed a lot and I truly appreciate your patience dealing with a man like me.

To my beautiful daughter Ryann, It is my hopes that through these pages you're able to understand the meaning of love and that one day someone special will show themselves more worthy then the pages you've inspired me to write for young ladies like yourself.

My Best friends, LaDarell Bester (Dee), Darrel Bolton and TJ Brown. I couldn't asked for a better support system then you guys. From the trials and tribulations that we've all shared with each other along the way to accomplishing and becoming what we are today. And I can't forget my sky patrol brother Donald Johnson. I think about you every day and take comfort in knowing that you are looking out for me from up above. I love you guys madly.

HOW THIS JOURNEY BEGAN

I reluctantly joined Twitter six years ago with the thought process that saving my details for times spent together in person was more meaningful. I didn't like the idea of narrating my life via technology. What if I started tweeting about it more than experiencing it? I was protective of my anonymity. The internet is a massive place, and people aren't always kind; did I really want to open my daily ramblings to critique?

It took quiet some time until I begun to "like" or better yet understand what I was actually doing on this site. Following the right people, re-tweeting the things that sparked my interest and joining in on the hash-tagged discussions that mattered most to me gave me a creative outlet.

I noticed a very popular trending topic of discussion where women where sharing notes of love to their future mates. Very few men joined in and something inside me clicked. Why not speak into existence the type of love, partner and wife I affirm, dream and pray to have. I gave significant time to it and began writing to "her" for an entire year.

Too many times I have read and heard that *whoever finds a wife has found a good thing*, so I've always felt like I needed to do something that no man has done before to find that special someone for **me**. So that's exactly what I did. I dedicated an entire 365 days of love notes and affirmations to my future love.

"I'm doing my work" as Iyanla Vanzant would suggest and now I pray that you enjoy taking this unconditional journey of love with me as well as be encouraged to share this love language of mine to attract great love in your life. P.S. I left room for you to write back...

JANUARY

ME WARE WO
"I SHALL MARRY YOU"
(SYMBOL OF COMMITMENT, PERSEVERANCE)

DAY 1

Today I begin my search for you. Wherever you are, whomever you are, whenever you are, I will find you... by God's mercy.

_____

_____

_____

_____

_____

_____

_____

_____

_____

_____

_____

DAY 2

In my life's journey, it's these chapters about finding you that I'll cherish the most. You ready? ☺

_____

_____

_____

_____

_____

_____

_____

_____

_____

_____

_____

DAY 3

God will always be first in my life.
_____

_____

_____

_____

_____

_____

_____

_____

_____

_____

_____

_____

_____

_____

_____

_____

DAY 4

My daughter is a very important part of my life.

_____
_____
_____
_____
_____
_____
_____
_____
_____
_____
_____
_____

DAY 5

<u>I have embraced many beautiful memories in my life, but the one I'll admire the most is when I meet you.</u>

_____

_____

_____

_____

_____

_____

_____

_____

_____

_____

_____

DAY 6

I'll never miss an opportunity to tell you that you are beautiful.

_____

_____

_____

_____

_____

_____

_____

_____

_____

_____

_____

_____

DAY 7

<u>My mother raised me extremely well. You have nothing to worry about.</u>

_____

_____

_____

_____

_____

_____

_____

_____

_____

_____

_____

_____

_____

DAY 8

Not a day goes by without you on my mind.

_____

_____

_____

_____

_____

_____

_____

_____

_____

_____

_____

_____

_____

DAY 9

To wake up and see your face would mean___
everything to me.___

___

___

___

___

___

___

___

___

___

___

___

___

___

___

DAY 10

On a scale from 1 to 10, you're a 9 and I'm the 1 that your missing.

_____

_____

_____

_____

_____

_____

_____

_____

_____

_____

_____

_____

DAY 11

Who you are is enough. #affirmation_____

_____

_____

_____

_____

_____

_____

_____

_____

_____

_____

_____

_____

_____

DAY 12

Your voice will be my favorite sound.

DAY 13

You had me at zero mutual friends.

DAY 14

Smiling for no reason is what happens when I think of you.

DAY 15

You fill the space between my heartbeats._____

DAY 16

I will never forget your birthday, the day we__
met, your favorite color, the first time we____
kissed, or your birth mark(s)._____

_____

_____

_____

_____

_____

_____

_____

_____

_____

_____

_____

DAY 17

<u>I promise to laugh at your jokes...even if they</u>
<u>aren't funny... at all.</u>

_____

_____

_____

_____

_____

_____

_____

_____

_____

_____

_____

_____

DAY 18

There will never be a room where you are not the most beautiful.

_____

_____

_____

_____

_____

_____

_____

_____

_____

_____

_____

_____

DAY 19

I will greet you with kisses every time we meet
and part.

DAY 20

<u>You will be the best thing that ever</u>
<u>happened to me, I can feel it.</u>

DAY 21

Although we have never met there are so____
many sacrifices I'm making for you._____

_____

_____

_____

_____

_____

_____

_____

_____

_____

_____

_____

_____

DAY 22

When I say "You", I also mean "Me", So Hear "WE." _____

_____

_____

_____

_____

_____

_____

_____

_____

_____

_____

_____

_____

DAY 23

I want to wake up to sun rays reflecting from
your cheeks.

DAY 24

Look, I don't know if there's only one person
on the planet you're supposed to be with.. But
when we're together it sure feels that way.

DAY 25

I don't want to be bound to you, I just want to love you.

_____

_____

_____

_____

_____

_____

_____

_____

_____

_____

_____

_____

DAY 26

In the grand scheme of things... You're the *grand* part.

_____

_____

_____

_____

_____

_____

_____

_____

_____

_____

_____

_____

DAY 27

<u>Believe in me and I'll be everything you need.</u>

_____

_____

_____

_____

_____

_____

_____

_____

_____

_____

_____

_____

_____

_____

DAY 28

I promise you this, no matter who enters your life before me, I will love you more than any of them.

DAY 29

Sometimes I get jealous thinking someone___
could make you happier than I could. Real___
Talk!_____

_____

_____

_____

_____

_____

_____

_____

_____

_____

_____

_____

DAY 30

I may not be your 1st love, 1st kiss, 1st sight, or 1st date. But I'm not in this to be your 1st anything baby... I just want to be your last!

DAY 31

<u>My first thought in the morning is always *you*.</u>

_____

_____

_____

_____

_____

_____

_____

_____

_____

_____

_____

_____

_____

_____

FEBUARY

ME WARE WO
"I SHALL MARRY YOU"
(SYMBOL OF COMMITMENT, PERSEVERANCE)

DAY 1

I will not get mad at you about everything
when I'm only just mad at you about one
thing.

DAY 2

I need a hug. Well, I actually need your hug.

_____

_____

_____

_____

_____

_____

_____

_____

_____

_____

_____

_____

_____

_____

DAY 3

<u>My love for you is so **THICK** it drips...</u>

DAY 4

I can't imagine ever tiring of your voice.

_____

_____

_____

_____

_____

_____

_____

_____

_____

_____

_____

_____

DAY 5

There will be days when all I need is your____
heartbeat against mine._____

_____

_____

_____

_____

_____

_____

_____

_____

_____

_____

_____

_____

DAY 6

May our minds always find a way to connect.

DAY 7

You will never have to worry about me raising a hand to you, except if it's to caress.

DAY 8

I got your back baby, just you wait and see.

_____

_____

_____

_____

_____

_____

_____

_____

_____

_____

_____

_____

DAY 9

My day starts at your voice.

_____

_____

_____

_____

_____

_____

_____

_____

_____

_____

_____

_____

_____

_____

DAY 10

You will never have to guess what's on my mind. I will tell you, even if I don't know.

_____

_____

_____

_____

_____

_____

_____

_____

_____

_____

_____

_____

DAY 11

When I get the chance to say I love you it____
means I see God in you and though I accept__
you as is without judgment, I actually hold___
you to the standard of deity._____

_____

_____

_____

_____

_____

_____

_____

_____

_____

_____

_____

DAY 12

I promise to hold your hand in public and kiss you even when all my friends are looking. It's all about us darling!

_____

_____

_____

_____

_____

_____

_____

_____

_____

_____

DAY 13

Good morning kisses on your forehead sounds
really good right now...
_____

_____

_____

_____

_____

_____

_____

_____

_____

_____

_____

_____

DAY 14

Crisp air. Chilled wine. Communication
deepens. Your my Valentine.

_____

_____

_____

_____

_____

_____

_____

_____

_____

_____

_____

DAY 15

<u>All I ask, **believe in me**</u>.

DAY 16

I want to kiss the morning sky off of your
collarbone._____

_____

_____

_____

_____

_____

_____

_____

_____

_____

_____

_____

DAY 17

Although it's not time yet, would you grab my arm so I can tell my friends I've been touched by an angel?

DAY 18

When the wind blows on me, I just hope it's__
pushing me closer and closer towards you.___

_____

_____

_____

_____

_____

_____

_____

_____

_____

_____

_____

DAY 19

You're seriously all I want._____

_____

_____

_____

_____

_____

_____

_____

_____

_____

_____

_____

_____

_____

_____

DAY 20

Wherever you are, may the midnight sky
cover you.

_____

_____

_____

_____

_____

_____

_____

_____

_____

_____

_____

_____

DAY 21

If you asked me how many times you have_
crossed my mind I would say once... Because_
the thought of you never really leaves._____

_____

_____

_____

_____

_____

_____

_____

_____

_____

_____

_____

DAY 22

I want you to love me but love God more.

_____

_____

_____

_____

_____

_____

_____

_____

_____

_____

_____

_____

DAY 23

We can ride the same wave as long as you give effort to keep us balanced.

_____

_____

_____

_____

_____

_____

_____

_____

_____

_____

_____

_____

_____

DAY 24

You are the picture God keeps in his wallet.

_____

_____

_____

_____

_____

_____

_____

_____

_____

_____

_____

_____

DAY 25

I love you so much that I'll eat the irregular
brown potato chip so you don't have to.

DAY 26

I will love you as if no one has destroyed you before.

_____

_____

_____

_____

_____

_____

_____

_____

_____

_____

_____

_____

DAY 27

<u>You are the dream the sun is having... That's</u>
<u>how beautiful you are to me.</u>

DAY 28

I pray to be worth your truth. #affirmation

_____

_____

_____

_____

_____

_____

_____

_____

_____

_____

_____

MARCH

ME WARE WO
"I SHALL MARRY YOU"
(SYMBOL OF COMMITMENT, PERSEVERANCE)

DAY 1

I just caught myself daydreaming about you.

_____

_____

_____

_____

_____

_____

_____

_____

_____

_____

_____

_____

DAY 2

I honestly can't remember the last time you__
were **NOT** on my mind._____

_____

_____

_____

_____

_____

_____

_____

_____

_____

_____

_____

_____

DAY 3

Wherever you are is where I want to be.

_____

_____

_____

_____

_____

_____

_____

_____

_____

_____

_____

_____

DAY 4

iloveyou; I wrote it with no spaces so there's__
no room for anyone else._____

DAY 5

God made you. Then He made me. Then He__
whispered 'meant to be.'

_____

_____

_____

_____

_____

_____

_____

_____

_____

_____

_____

_____

DAY 6

 NothingcancomebetweenUS. _#affirmation

_____

_____

_____

_____

_____

_____

_____

_____

_____

_____

_____

_____

_____

DAY 7

You will never be weak to me for shedding a__
tear. Shoot, I may even shed a few too if the__
occasion calls._____

_____

_____

_____

_____

_____

_____

_____

_____

_____

_____

_____

DAY 8

I want to be the sponsor of your smile. _____

_____

_____

_____

_____

_____

_____

_____

_____

_____

_____

_____

_____

DAY 9

You take me. I take you, and in this_____
partnership comes everlasting love._____

_____

_____

_____

_____

_____

_____

_____

_____

_____

_____

_____

_____

DAY 10

Light._____

Love._____

Solace._____

Comfort._____

Warmth._____

Shelter._____

Support._____

Strength._____

Hope._____

Humor._____

Song._____

All offered here... #affirmation_____

_____

_____

_____

_____

DAY 11

Know that I won't say 'I love you' just to hear
it back. I'll say it to make sure you know.

_____

_____

_____

_____

_____

_____

_____

_____

_____

_____

_____

_____

DAY 12

I love you because the entire universe
conspired to help me find you.

_____

_____

_____

_____

_____

_____

_____

_____

_____

_____

_____

_____

_____

DAY 13

My heart has the perfect picture of you, but it won't expect you to be perfect.

DAY 14

Trust me...

DAY 15

What butterflies? I feel the entire zoo in my stomach when I see you.

_____

_____

_____

_____

_____

_____

_____

_____

_____

_____

_____

_____

DAY 16

I really admire how you dress fly and exhibit__
swagger without losing your modesty in the__
process._____

_____

_____

_____

_____

_____

_____

_____

_____

_____

_____

_____

_____

DAY 17

Yesterday's love note to you is turning me on right now. ☺

_____

_____

_____

_____

_____

_____

_____

_____

_____

_____

_____

DAY 18

_Your height. Your weight. Your kisses. Your words. Your heart. Your laugh. Your body.___ Your scent. Your soul. Everything about You!_

_____

_____

_____

_____

_____

_____

_____

_____

_____

_____

_____

DAY 19

You really smooth out my rough edges.

_____

_____

_____

_____

_____

_____

_____

_____

_____

_____

_____

_____

DAY 20

The moment you allowed me to bless the food you prepared for me I knew.

_____

_____

_____

_____

_____

_____

_____

_____

_____

_____

_____

_____

DAY 21

_The look in your eyes when I wake you up___ will erase any unnecessary emotion I may have been feeling._____

_____

_____

_____

_____

_____

_____

_____

_____

_____

_____

_____

DAY 22

I will learn to interpret your silence.

DAY 23

I can't believe that I'm your man and I get to kiss you just because I can.

_____

_____

_____

_____

_____

_____

_____

_____

_____

_____

_____

DAY 24

I want to feel past your skin into your energy.

_____

_____

_____

_____

_____

_____

_____

_____

_____

_____

_____

_____

DAY 25

_I promise I will redefine your concept of____
LOVE._____

_____

_____

_____

_____

_____

_____

_____

_____

_____

_____

_____

_____

DAY 26

Sometimes I'm gonna need some alone time. Just me and God. I know you'll understand... Right?_____

_____
_____
_____
_____
_____
_____
_____
_____
_____
_____
_____
_____

DAY 27

Tears are words the heart can't express. Go ahead cry, I understand you all the same.

_____

_____

_____

_____

_____

_____

_____

_____

_____

_____

_____

_____

DAY 28

Good morning, *Gorgeous!!!*

_____

_____

_____

_____

_____

_____

_____

_____

_____

_____

_____

_____

DAY 29

I think about *you*, therefore **you** exist.

_____

_____

_____

_____

_____

_____

_____

_____

_____

_____

_____

_____

_____

_____

DAY 30

_The moments I see you doing something...__
walk up behind you and put my arms around_
you will be special._____

_____

_____

_____

_____

_____

_____

_____

_____

_____

_____

_____*at least for me...*_

DAY 31

 I can honestly say the more that we spend time... I'm attracted to you darling, your body, soul and mind.

_____

_____

_____

_____

_____

_____

_____

_____

_____

_____

_____

APRIL

ME WARE WO
"I SHALL MARRY YOU"
(SYMBOL OF COMMITMENT, PERSEVERANCE)

DAY 1

Now, about that cookie?!? ☺

_____

_____

_____

_____

_____

_____

_____

_____

_____

_____

_____

_____

_____

_____

DAY 2

Meet me at the gym, so I know it's real!

DAY 3

I do have female friends...but only one female I'm in love with...YOU!

DAY 4

"Come here girl and give me the luscious."

_____

_____

_____

_____

_____

_____

_____

_____

_____

_____

_____

_____

_____

_____

DAY 5

If people are truly, madly, deeply in love with each other, they will find a way... Let's always find a way Ok?_____

_____

_____

_____

_____

_____

_____

_____

_____

_____

_____

DAY 6

 Sometimes I feel like my heart knows exactly where to find you.

DAY 7

_Sometimes I feel like I need you more than__
the next breath I take._____

_____
_____
_____
_____
_____
_____
_____
_____
_____
_____
_____
_____
_____

DAY 8

 I took a sip of yo tea and ain't been right
eva since.

DAY 9

 The thing about giving away your heart is
that you never get the whole thing back, only
pieces...and in some cases, nothing at all.
I guess what I'm trying to say is... If you're
trying, I'm willing!

DAY 10

I know telling you you're beautiful does no
good if I'm not making you feel beautiful. So,
today let me run your bath and massage the
pain away.

DAY 11

_Everything happens in its time.. I love when
*"It's Time"*_____

_____

_____

_____

_____

_____

_____

_____

_____

_____

_____

_____

DAY 12

I'm in love with "The Creator" in you.

_____

_____

_____

_____

_____

_____

_____

_____

_____

_____

_____

_____

DAY 13

Have I crossed your mind today.. If I did... I
wonder if you smiled.

_____

_____

_____

_____

_____

_____

_____

_____

_____

_____

_____

DAY 14

 Wherever you are in the world right now,
"goodnight beautiful." I can't wait to tell you
that in person and kiss you.

_____

_____

_____

_____

_____

_____

_____

_____

_____

_____

_____

_____

DAY 15

I like the left side of the bed.

DAY 16

_You're going to have one amazing husband! #affirmation_____

_____

_____

_____

_____

_____

_____

_____

_____

_____

_____

_____

DAY 17

Can you take the spray in the bathroom when you go. I'm just saying.

DAY 18

Challenge me to be better for you & me..._____

_____

_____

_____

_____

_____

_____

_____

_____

_____

_____

_____

_____

_____

_____

DAY 19

_I can't wait for the days that we call in sick to work together._____

_____

_____

_____

_____

_____

_____

_____

_____

_____

_____

_____

_____

DAY 20

There will be 3 of us in this relationship: God, You & me.

_____

_____

_____

_____

_____

_____

_____

_____

_____

_____

_____

_____

DAY 21

_I promise to talk to you when things are____
bothering me instead of allowing it to build__
up._____

_____

_____

_____

_____

_____

_____

_____

_____

_____

_____

_____

DAY 22

 I'll work to make you fall in love with me all
over again at least once a week by doing the
little things that make your heart smile.

_____

_____

_____

_____

_____

_____

_____

_____

_____

_____

_____

DAY 23

_Thank you for remaining connected to my__
spirit._

DAY 24

Be who you say you are. That's what I'll love
about you most._____

_____

_____

_____

_____

_____

_____

_____

_____

_____

_____

_____

DAY 25

_**Love**. **Support**. _Affection_. It's right here_
waiting for you.

_____

_____

_____

_____

_____

_____

_____

_____

_____

_____

_____

_____

_____

DAY 26

I pray that you'll be a beautiful whisper
gently following me to sleep.

DAY 27

I write today because the thought of *"till death do us part"* is etched upon my soul.

DAY 28

All of me for all of you... Even trade.

DAY 29

I can't promise to fix all your problems, but I can promise you won't have to face them alone.

_____

_____

_____

_____

_____

_____

_____

_____

_____

_____

DAY 30

I could use a whole lot of YOU right now.

MAY

ME WARE WO
"I SHALL MARRY YOU"
(SYMBOL OF COMMITMENT, PERSEVERANCE)

DAY 1

 Don't ever think I fell for you, or fell over
you. I never did fall in love... I rose in it! and
will continue to rise in what we build.

_____

_____

_____

_____

_____

_____

_____

_____

_____

_____

_____

DAY 2

There is an empty space in the middle of my
chest that only you fill._____

_____

_____

_____

_____

_____

_____

_____

_____

_____

_____

_____

_____

DAY 3

_You are all the things I never knew I needed.

_____

_____

_____

_____

_____

_____

_____

_____

_____

_____

_____

_____

_____

DAY 4

I want to be your favorite hello and your hardest goodbye.

DAY 5

I can't wait to breathe your fragrance.

_____

_____

_____

_____

_____

_____

_____

_____

_____

_____

_____

_____

_____

DAY 6

It's date night! Let's act like we just met.

DAY 7

Your my four letter word. #affirmation

_____

_____

_____

_____

_____

_____

_____

_____

_____

_____

_____

_____

_____

DAY 8

_Just so we're clear, I do the proposing!_____
Proverbs 18:22 states "He who finds a wife____
finds what is good and receives favor from the
Lord."_____

_____

_____

_____

_____

_____

_____

_____

_____

_____

_____

_____

DAY 9

The way you walk completely owns my pulse.

_____

_____

_____

_____

_____

_____

_____

_____

_____

_____

_____

_____

_____

DAY 10

You are my fulfilled wish. #affirmation

_____

_____

_____

_____

_____

_____

_____

_____

_____

_____

_____

_____

DAY 11

There's a lack of you & an overabundance of me in this bed.

DAY 12

 I like that your clothes are tight enough to
show you're a woman, but loose enough to
show you're a lady.

_____

_____

_____

_____

_____

_____

_____

_____

_____

_____

_____

DAY 13

_I'll never discourage you from doing what___
you believe in...I'll be one of your greatest____
supporters._____

_____

_____

_____

_____

_____

_____

_____

_____

_____

_____

_____

DAY 14

I love yoga pants.

_____

_____

_____

_____

_____

_____

_____

_____

_____

_____

_____

_____

your yoga pants....

DAY 15

 _The mistakes I'm making now are life lessons
that continue to teach me how to get it right_
with you._____

_____

_____

_____

_____

_____

_____

_____

_____

_____

_____

_____

DAY 16

 Finding you will be one of my greatest
testimonies of how great is our God.

_____

_____

_____

_____

_____

_____

_____

_____

_____

_____

_____

_____

DAY 17

Encourage me. Push me. Keep me in check.
Tell me when I'm wrong. Praise God with me.
Read with/to me. Love me._____

_____

_____

_____

_____

_____

_____

_____

_____

_____

_____

_____

DAY 18

I like the right side of the bed too...

_____

_____

_____

_____

_____

_____

_____

_____

_____

_____

_____

_____

DAY 19

I'll get jealous at times when another guy hugs you...Because for a second, he had my entire world in his arms.

DAY 20

Stay up with me and talk about nothing.

DAY 21

Sing with me

She answered in whispers soft

We'll listen in awe

#haiku

DAY 22

_Our wedding day will be about celebrating__ how beautiful you are and how lucky I am.___

DAY 23

I'm only as healthy as you are...When you're
sick, I'm sick.

DAY 24

_We can't hear if we're both talking...Let's_____
just listen so we learn as we love._Capeesh?__

_____

_____

_____

_____

_____

_____

_____

_____

_____

_____

_____

_____

_____

DAY 25

Our code for truce: Kiss on the forehead

_____

_____

_____

_____

_____

_____

_____

_____

_____

_____

_____

_____

_____

DAY 26

 We will always have God, in the good and
the bad. He is our provider and protector.

_____

_____

_____

_____

_____

_____

_____

_____

_____

_____

_____

_____

DAY 27

 At least once a night I will try to synchronize my breathing to yours.

DAY 28

Open, close, opened once more... I will rush
through every blink to lay my eyes on you.___

DAY 29

 Listen to Kem "Love never fails" with me
when times get hard.

DAY 30

I can be wrong every time there is a disagreement as long as we do the right thing to make things work/last.

_____

_____

_____

_____

_____

_____

_____

_____

_____

_____

_____

DAY 31

_I'm. Really. Glad. To. Have. You. In. My. Life.
#affirmation_____

_____

_____

_____

_____

_____

_____

_____

_____

_____

_____

_____

JUNE

ME WARE WO
"I SHALL MARRY YOU"
(SYMBOL OF COMMITMENT, PERSEVERANCE)

DAY 1

 Our individual strengths and spiritual____
maturity will combine to make one hell of a
power couple._____

_____

_____

_____

_____

_____

_____

_____

_____

_____

_____

DAY 2

Tell me directly what's bothering you.

_____

_____

_____

_____

_____

_____

_____

_____

_____

_____

_____

_____

DAY 3

_I love to look at you under the dim lights but it's what I can't see that keeps me going._____

DAY 4

You **magnify** my better half.. #affirmation

DAY 5

_For every reason in the world there is to quit, I want '*you*' to be the only reason to keep____ going._____

_____

_____

_____

_____

_____

_____

_____

_____

_____

_____

_____

_____

DAY 6

_I don't sleep on couches. #affirmation_____

_____

_____

_____

_____

_____

_____

_____

_____

_____

_____

_____

_____

_____

DAY 7

 I just want to curl up with you and listen to
your heartbeat...Before and after.

_____

_____

_____

_____

_____

_____

_____

_____

_____

_____

_____

_____

DAY 8

WE *BOTH* DESERVE *EACH OTHERS* LOVE.

_____

_____

_____

_____

_____

_____

_____

_____

_____

_____

_____

_____

_____

_____

DAY 9

 In the perfect light at the right angle, let's
make our reflections dance.

DAY 10

You're the only *you* and I'm the only *I* when I say "I Love You."

DAY 11

<u>When days seem like your drowning, I'll pull the air from my lungs and place it in yours.</u>

_____

_____

_____

_____

_____

_____

_____

_____

_____

_____

_____

_____

DAY 12

_I hope that the words that I'm writing you so far have the strength in their wings to find its' way to you_____

_____

_____

_____

_____

_____

_____

_____

_____

_____

_____

_____

DAY 13

_These arms of mine will worship and adore__
you with all its being._____

_____

_____

_____

_____

_____

_____

_____

_____

_____

_____

_____

_____

DAY 14

_With every single part of me... My love for__
you is constantly forever and ever on repeat.__

DAY 15

All I need is *YOU* needing me.

DAY 16

I long for the days my heart and your soul go bump in the night.

_____

_____

_____

_____

_____

_____

_____

_____

_____

_____

_____

_____

DAY 17

I don't mind being lost when I end up finding myself in your thoughts.

_____

_____

_____

_____

_____

_____

_____

_____

_____

_____

_____

_____

DAY 18

Sometimes your words are exactly what I
need to hear.

_____

_____

_____

_____

_____

_____

_____

_____

_____

_____

_____

_____

DAY 19

I dreamt we shared a kiss and called it home.

_____

_____

_____

_____

_____

_____

_____

_____

_____

_____

_____

_____

_____

DAY 20

I WANT TO SEE YOU WIN... #affirmation

DAY 21

I want a relationship with no gender roles: we both grind, we both pay, we're both romantic and we both spoil each other.

DAY 22

There is not one thing that I will would not
do for you to see you smile._____

_____

_____

_____

_____

_____

_____

_____

_____

_____

_____

_____

DAY 23

 I long to kiss you on your neck and make the rhythm of my breath cause your skin to crawl.

_____

_____

_____

_____

_____

_____

_____

_____

_____

_____

_____

_____

DAY 24

 I love every sound you don't even know you make when you're sleeping next to me.

DAY 25

No distance in this life or the next that'll keep me from finding you.

_____

_____

_____

_____

_____

_____

_____

_____

_____

_____

_____

_____

_____

DAY 26

I love the music composed by your body moving between the sheets.

DAY 27

If you treat me right, I'll treat you better.

DAY 28

An "I miss you" text from you right now would be great.

_____

_____

_____

_____

_____

_____

_____

_____

_____

_____

_____

_____

DAY 29

I dream about the first time we kiss after
spending so much time apart...

_____

_____

_____

_____

_____

_____

_____

_____

_____

_____

_____

_____

_____

DAY 30

 I ache for you in places I never knew existed.

JULY

ME WARE WO
"I SHALL MARRY YOU"
(SYMBOL OF COMMITMENT, PERSEVERANCE)

DAY 1

When we're together, nothing else matters to me.

DAY 2

Your smile is one the sexist curves on your body.

DAY 3

Let's help the environment by saving water and shower together...

_____

_____

_____

_____

_____

_____

_____

_____

_____

_____

_____

DAY 4

Be my firework

Be my spark

I burn for you

With. All. My. Heart

#micropoetry

DAY 5

You are every wish, on every star, in every dream I'm having today.

DAY 6

Until we kiss I AM not real...

_____

_____

_____

_____

_____

_____

_____

_____

_____

_____

_____

_____

_____

_____

DAY 7

You're the only one I'm calling babe, nobody else.

DAY 8

My lips are craving a quick vacation to the small of your back.

_____
_____
_____
_____
_____
_____
_____
_____
_____
_____
_____
_____

DAY 9

_Cuddling with you is the best feeling in the world._____

_____

_____

_____

_____

_____

_____

_____

_____

_____

_____

_____

DAY 10

You have no idea the aching in my heart when I can't find you.

_____

_____

_____

_____

_____

_____

_____

_____

_____

_____

_____

_____

DAY 11

 I'll always kiss you like that is the only thing
I'm allowed to do.

DAY 12

_Between then and now are all the perfect___
moment's that lock me in to finding you.___

_____

_____

_____

_____

_____

_____

_____

_____

_____

_____

_____

_____

_____

DAY 13

There are so many beautiful reasons to be happy. You reading my love note today is now added to the list.

_____

_____

_____

_____

_____

_____

_____

_____

_____

_____

_____

DAY 14

 You are so much more than my heart ever believed it deserved.

_____

_____

_____

_____

_____

_____

_____

_____

_____

_____

_____

_____

_____

DAY 15

You skin is so beautiful that if I were any smaller I would explore the tiny lines covering your palms.

DAY 16

_I long to lay in bed with you,.. Lifting the covers to your shoulders, while kissing you to sleep.

DAY 17

You're my favorite passenger aboard every train of thought in my mind.

DAY 18

Everything you've secretly prayed for,.. I have inside of me. #affirmation_____

_____

_____

_____

_____

_____

_____

_____

_____

_____

_____

_____

_____

DAY 19

_I hope you're my friend forever because that's how long I'm going to need you!_____

_____

_____

_____

_____

_____

_____

_____

_____

_____

_____

_____

_____

DAY 20

I need you in my life the way a person drowning needs air.

DAY 21

I think about you anytime anything around me is even remotely beautiful.

DAY 22

 I don't care how hard it is when we get on each other's nerves. Nothing is worse than being apart from you.

DAY 23

_You and I will make the perfect team.
#affirmation_____

_____

_____

_____

_____

_____

_____

_____

_____

_____

_____

_____

DAY 24

I'm gonna love being loved by you...

_____

_____

_____

_____

_____

_____

_____

_____

_____

_____

_____

_____

_____

DAY 25

Yes, your way of thinking means everything
to me, us & our future together

_____

_____

_____

_____

_____

_____

_____

_____

_____

_____

_____

_____

DAY 26

If kissing you were like raindrops, we would create thunderstorms.

_____

_____

_____

_____

_____

_____

_____

_____

_____

_____

_____

_____

DAY 27

The mere thought of our union pierces my soul.

DAY 28

I can't find the words today to express the disbelief that I haven't found you yet.

_____

_____

_____

_____

_____

_____

_____

_____

_____

_____

_____

_____

DAY 29

Let's go for a romantic walk that never ends.

_____

_____

_____

_____

_____

_____

_____

_____

_____

_____

_____

_____

_____

DAY 30

_Saying how much I love you has a more delicious sound between kissing your lips.__

_____

_____

_____

_____

_____

_____

_____

_____

_____

_____

_____

_____

DAY 31

The truth is, if I could be with anyone, I would still choose this search for you.

_____

_____

_____

_____

_____

_____

_____

_____

_____

_____

_____

_____

AUGUST

ME WARE WO
"I SHALL MARRY YOU"
(SYMBOL OF COMMITMENT, PERSEVERANCE)

DAY 1

I want you... I want us.. I want it all... With you.. Only you.

_____

_____

_____

_____

_____

_____

_____

_____

_____

_____

_____

_____

DAY 2

 The only perfect I could ever pray to be is perfect for you.

DAY 3

The moment I understand exactly how your mind works, we will not need words.

_____

_____

_____

_____

_____

_____

_____

_____

_____

_____

_____

_____

DAY 4

I can't wait to give you my famous back massage.

_____

_____

_____

_____

_____

_____

_____

_____

_____

_____

_____

_____

DAY 5

Spooning will become our talking, as our bodies curled into apostrophes, with no words between...

DAY 6

I'll carry your heart in mine when we are
apart.

_____

_____

_____

_____

_____

_____

_____

_____

_____

_____

_____

_____

DAY 7

_The moment you ask me which is more important, "you or my life?" I'll say without a doubt "my life" because you will know that "You.Are.My.Life"_____

_____

_____

_____

_____

_____

_____

_____

_____

_____

_____

DAY 8

The crease of my dimples have waited its whole life to be filled by your nose.

_____

_____

_____

_____

_____

_____

_____

_____

_____

_____

_____

_____

DAY 9

If you held up a single rose into a mirror, you'd be looking at 2 of the most beautiful things in the world... My world.

_____

_____

_____

_____

_____

_____

_____

_____

_____

_____

_____

DAY 10

_When you look into my eyes you'll find me, but when you look into my heart you'll find you.

_____

_____

_____

_____

_____

_____

_____

_____

_____

_____

_____

_____

DAY 11

Sometimes I wonder how did a guy like me end up with a queen like you...

_____

_____

_____

_____

_____

_____

_____

_____

_____

_____

_____

_____

DAY 12

I could hold you forever.

_____

_____

_____

_____

_____

_____

_____

_____

_____

_____

_____

_____

_____

DAY 13

"noh ss!w !"

(read it upside down)

_____

_____

_____

_____

_____

_____

_____

_____

_____

_____

_____

_____

_____

_____

_____

DAY 14

When you feel the wind blow, face into it and listen. I'll be whispering "I love you."

DAY 15

I'll stand between anything that brings you harm.

DAY 16

You are a manifestation of all of my most memorable dreams.

_____

_____

_____

_____

_____

_____

_____

_____

_____

_____

_____

_____

_____

DAY 17

My heart is fine with a woman like you in it.

_____

_____

_____

_____

_____

_____

_____

_____

_____

_____

_____

_____

_____

DAY 18

 Forgive my lips for they know exactly what they want to do to you.

DAY 19

_The breath in my lungs are passionately waiting for you to steal them._____

_____

_____

_____

_____

_____

_____

_____

_____

_____

_____

_____

_____

_____

DAY 20

 Before I met you I never knew what it was like to smile for no reason at all.

_____

_____

_____

_____

_____

_____

_____

_____

_____

_____

_____

_____

DAY 21

_You absolutely, positively *do not* look fat in that outfit.

DAY 22

All I ever needed is in your eyes.

DAY 23

I don't just love you... I'm in the love you.

DAY 24

 I'll ask, because I respect hearing your side of things. I'll share, because I like including you in all of who I AM and I'll care because it's You.

_____

_____

_____

_____

_____

_____

_____

_____

_____

_____

DAY 25

_On this day, I just wanted to let you know that you're all I've ever wanted in a woman. I love you. Truly. Madly. Deeply._____

_____

_____

_____

_____

_____

_____

_____

_____

_____

_____

_____

DAY 26

If all we can have is forever then I think we should start right now.

DAY 27

I know I said this once before, but I really do love "The Creator" in you.

DAY 28

 All these things I seem to just go through. It would ease my pain, if I could just have you.

DAY 29

You are what I need in my life... #affirmation_

_____

_____

_____

_____

_____

_____

_____

_____

_____

_____

_____

_____

DAY 30

____Your smile makes me laugh._____

____Your laugh makes me smile._____

DAY 31

My favorite part of this story is when you walk into my life.

_____
_____
_____
_____
_____
_____
_____
_____
_____
_____
_____

SEPTEMBER

ME WARE WO
"I SHALL MARRY YOU"
(SYMBOL OF COMMITMENT, PERSEVERANCE)

DAY 1

My search for you has shown me how much love I have to give. Now you get to take it all!

_____

_____

_____

_____

_____

_____

_____

_____

_____

_____

_____

DAY 2

_There are these random moments when I___
suddenly stop doing what I'm doing and go off
to a place that gives me a sense of calm, quite,
warm peace. I just realized, these are the____
moments I spend thinking about you._____

DAY 3

You are my life. When I close my eyes, I can feel your presence.

DAY 4

My love for you is a journey worth packing
for...

———————————————————

———————————————————

———————————————————

———————————————————

———————————————————

———————————————————

———————————————————

———————————————————

———————————————————

———————————————————

———————————————————

———————————————————

DAY 5

Your faith and belief in me is nothing short of my everything.

DAY 6

I've never, till now, had a woman who could give me rest. I love you so very much.

_____

_____

_____

_____

_____

_____

_____

_____

_____

_____

_____

DAY 7

 My life seems to pause at times when you're not around.

DAY 8

 I want you to know that love is my other religion. I have faith in you... in us!

_____

_____

_____

_____

_____

_____

_____

_____

_____

_____

_____

_____

DAY 9

 Knowing that we aren't going to be perfect in this relationship, I'll do my best to understand every word you are NOT saying._____

_____

_____

_____

_____

_____

_____

_____

_____

_____

_____

_____

DAY 10

_Accept me without change and watch me___
fulfill 'The List."_____

_____

_____

_____

_____

_____

_____

_____

_____

_____

_____

_____

_____

_____

DAY 11

It is the good times and it is the not so good times that will tie us together.

DAY 12

 Lean towards me so I can whisper in your ear all of the places my lips are going to kiss._____

_____

_____

_____

_____

_____

_____

_____

_____

_____

_____

_____

_____

DAY 13

Lay in my lap as I read the next chapters of our life.

_____

_____

_____

_____

_____

_____

_____

_____

_____

_____

_____

_____

DAY 14

I love how you flirt with me in public as if no one else is around.

DAY 15

My worst day with you trumps my best day without you.

_____

_____

_____

_____

_____

_____

_____

_____

_____

_____

_____

_____

DAY 16

I go to sleep every night thinking of you by my side.

_____

_____

_____

_____

_____

_____

_____

_____

_____

_____

_____

_____

DAY 17

_The fact that I feel much better when your__
around lets me know you're the one._____

_____

_____

_____

_____

_____

_____

_____

_____

_____

_____

_____

_____

DAY 18

 I'll never miss an opportunity to tell you how much you mean to me. (Hint: This Book) ☺

DAY 19

You're my sweetest temptation. #affirmation

DAY 20

 If I could describe you in two words, I'd call you "**My Air**."

_____

_____

_____

_____

_____

_____

_____

_____

_____

_____

_____

_____

DAY 21

_I wish you could hear how you got my heart racing... Like a soul clap..._____

_____

_____

_____

_____

_____

_____

_____

_____

_____

_____

_____

_____

_____

DAY 22

I have a crush on your *mouth.*

DAY 23

I'm not here to hurt you, baby I'm just here to please you.

DAY 24

Can't you tell the way I love you, touching you the way that I do?

_____

_____

_____

_____

_____

_____

_____

_____

_____

_____

_____

_____

DAY 25

_I'm the answer to all your heart's questions.
It's always been me and only me!_

_____

_____

_____

_____

_____

_____

_____

_____

_____

_____

_____

_____

DAY 26

The fact that you give me the strength, faith, and never ending courage to be myself, makes me feel like I can conquer the world.

_____

_____

_____

_____

_____

_____

_____

_____

_____

_____

_____

_____

DAY 27

I thank God for you every morning, noon, and night.

DAY 28

Whenever your 'walls' go up, I'll be the best climber you have ever seen.

DAY 29

I know that I'm getting close to finding you because I can feel you in my heart and hear you in my thoughts.

_____

_____

_____

_____

_____

_____

_____

_____

_____

_____

DAY 30

<u>You are the beautiful chaos that lives inside my soul.</u>

OCTOBER

ME WARE WO
"I SHALL MARRY YOU"
(SYMBOL OF COMMITMENT, PERSEVERANCE)

DAY 1

 You are the only woman to ever make me daydream of the future... ***Our future***.

_____

_____

_____

_____

_____

_____

_____

_____

_____

_____

_____

_____

DAY 2

_Being under the influence of your love is my ultimate high.

DAY 3

It's just us against the world... You & me girl! #affirmation

_____

_____

_____

_____

_____

_____

_____

_____

_____

_____

_____

_____

_____

DAY 4

When I think of home, it's not a place or a thing... It's having my arms around your waist and never letting go.

DAY 5

It is through your faith in me that I learned
to be the man I was meant to be... and for that
I say Thank You!!!

_____

_____

_____

_____

_____

_____

_____

_____

_____

_____

_____

DAY 6

There's a part of me that's going to be in love with you for the rest of our life.

DAY 7

Our first kiss could take a while... #jussayin

_____

_____

_____

_____

_____

_____

_____

_____

_____

_____

_____

_____

_____

_____

DAY 8

The best thing about me has always been the idea of you.

_____

_____

_____

_____

_____

_____

_____

_____

_____

_____

_____

_____

DAY 9

I'm so infatuated of who you are.

DAY 10

Me wishing to see you... Right at this very moment... Literally, at this very second. That's how much I want to be with you...

DAY 11

 You'll believe in us both by the time that I
am through.

DAY 12

When I talk to you, my day gets a whole lot better.

_____

_____

_____

_____

_____

_____

_____

_____

_____

_____

_____

_____

DAY 13

I'll remember everything you think I forgot.

_____

_____

_____

_____

_____

_____

_____

_____

_____

_____

_____

_____

DAY 14

I'll get jealous.

I'll get mad.

I'll get worried.

I'll get curious.

All of that is only because I love you.

DAY 15

Ain't no other woman I want, *"You Put It On Me."*

DAY 16

My best ideas will come from your heart.

DAY 17

 I adore you in every way that a man can adore a woman.

DAY 18

I'll catch you if you fall...

_____

_____

_____

_____

_____

_____

_____

_____

_____

_____

_____

_____

DAY 19

It's impossible to be in a bad mood when I'm
around you.

DAY 20

_Nooo!!! baby it's not burnt; I like my food Cajun style.

DAY 21

I always put the seat down!!!

_____

_____

_____

_____

_____

_____

_____

_____

_____

_____

_____

_____

_____

_____

DAY 22

Baby, you are my true meaning of happiness.

_____

_____

_____

_____

_____

_____

_____

_____

_____

_____

_____

_____

DAY 23

Psst! Look at the stars tonight. Watch how they'll shine for you.

DAY 24

I like it when you kiss me to sleep.

DAY 25

I have a million thoughts wrapped around a
single word... **YOU!!!**

DAY 26

_Let us count the stars and intertwine our legs together as we fall asleep. Sweet dreams_____ gorgeous!_____

_____

_____

_____

_____

_____

_____

_____

_____

_____

_____

_____

DAY 27

I'll hold you in my calm & bathe you in my kisses.

DAY 28

_I've waited so long to wake up on this morning and unwrap your love.

_____

_____

_____

_____

_____

_____

_____

_____

_____

_____

_____

DAY 29

 You and only you will ever fit with me and only me.

DAY 30

Of all the wishes in all of my life, the only one that will forever remain is you.

DAY 31

I'm haunted by your beautiful face without mine... Filling the frames of photos by my bed.

NOVEMBER

ME WARE WO
"I SHALL MARRY YOU"
(SYMBOL OF COMMITMENT, PERSEVERANCE)

DAY 1

_You make me so much more than I ever
was._____

_____

_____

_____

_____

_____

_____

_____

_____

_____

_____

_____

_____

DAY 2

_The way I can smell you in my collar... It's a great feeling... To know that you are with me.

———————————————————

———————————————————

———————————————————

———————————————————

———————————————————

———————————————————

———————————————————

———————————————————

———————————————————

———————————————————

———————————————————

———————————————————

DAY 3

If I completely lose my mind it will be your name I mumble into the madness.

_____

_____

_____

_____

_____

_____

_____

_____

_____

_____

_____

_____

DAY 4

I want every single inch of your skin covered
by my lips.

_____

_____

_____

_____

_____

_____

_____

_____

_____

_____

_____

_____

DAY 5

_There will be compositions of music in us waiting to be played aloud. Can you hear it?__

DAY 6

_We can make it through anything as long as we always trust God.

_____

_____

_____

_____

_____

_____

_____

_____

_____

_____

_____

_____

DAY 7

I love those weekends waking up to you cooking breakfast in my shirt.

DAY 8

_I love you to the moon & beyond but sometimes you test my patience.

#KissOnForehead

DAY 9

I love that you still melt when I wink at you.

_____

_____

_____

_____

_____

_____

_____

_____

_____

_____

_____

_____

_____

DAY 10

I love the idea of becoming your husband
and knowing that I'm going to get to spend_
every single second having a good time with_
my best friend._____

_____

_____

_____

_____

_____

_____

_____

_____

_____

_____

DAY 11

Love is... coming home in a bad mood and instantly feeling better the moment that you kiss me.

DAY 12

_Know that when I'm being a little stubborn, It has nothing to do with you. I can be a little difficult sometimes. #realtalk

DAY 13

 I'm really bad about stealing all the covers at night.

DAY 14

I hope you have a very convincing *fake* laugh because I tend to think I'm funnier than I actually am.

DAY 15

Sometimes I like to dance in the middle of the street.

_____

_____

_____

_____

_____

_____

_____

_____

_____

_____

_____

_____

DAY 16

I'm kind of addicted to your kisses. Come here!

DAY 17

I may be strong but I dig knowing that you'll always be there if I need you.

_____

_____

_____

_____

_____

_____

_____

_____

_____

_____

_____

_____

DAY 18

Eyes closed, opened, closed again... My mind cannot help thinking you are the one for me.

DAY 19

Can you feel my arms stealing your feet from the ground to carry you home?

_____

_____

_____

_____

_____

_____

_____

_____

_____

_____

_____

_____

_____

DAY 20

When I think of you, I can't help but be reminded of all the mountains we're about to move.

_____

_____

_____

_____

_____

_____

_____

_____

_____

_____

_____

_____

DAY 21

When I think about love, my thoughts **begin** and **end** with *you*.

DAY 22

You *amaze* me.

DAY 23

 Our love will be so different from anything we've ever experienced before... satisfying, genuine, and pure... untainted by attitudes, blame and insecurities.

_____

_____

_____

_____

_____

_____

_____

_____

_____

_____

_____

DAY 24

_The fact that you own my smile, and will always have my utmost unconditional love. Selah!_____

_____

_____

_____

_____

_____

_____

_____

_____

_____

_____

_____

_____

DAY 25

I promise not to forget where I love from.

_____

_____

_____

_____

_____

_____

_____

_____

_____

_____

_____

_____

_____

DAY 26

Between you and the universe, I'd choose you... because you're my universe and that would make me lose absolutely nothing at all.

_____

_____

_____

_____

_____

_____

_____

_____

_____

_____

_____

DAY 27

_You are my lover and my friend. I treasure each side, just as I have treasured our life together._____

_____

_____

_____

_____

_____

_____

_____

_____

_____

_____

DAY 28

There will be other books, but you will forever be my 1st story.

_____

_____

_____

_____

_____

_____

_____

_____

_____

_____

_____

_____

DAY 29

I just wanna laugh with you. No arguing, no talking work, no me me me or you you you... just laugh about silly things. You know?!?____

_____

_____

_____

_____

_____

_____

_____

_____

_____

_____

_____

_____

DAY 30

I hope when I do the *"little things"* it occupies the "BIGGEST PART" of your heart.

_____

_____

_____

_____

_____

_____

_____

_____

_____

_____

_____

_____

DECEMBER

ME WARE WO
"I SHALL MARRY YOU"
(SYMBOL OF COMMITMENT, PERSEVERANCE)

DAY 1

<u>You are the most beautiful story behind the emotion of love in my heart.</u>

_____

_____

_____

_____

_____

_____

_____

_____

_____

_____

_____

_____

DAY 2

Did I mention I love yoga pants?

your yoga pants..

DAY 3

You're worth so much more than anything I can write you today.

_____

_____

_____

_____

_____

_____

_____

_____

_____

_____

_____

DAY 4

You and me together make a beautiful "US."

_____

_____

_____

_____

_____

_____

_____

_____

_____

_____

_____

_____

_____

DAY 5

You make me feel tall & powerful...

_____

_____

_____

_____

_____

_____

_____

_____

_____

_____

_____

_____

DAY 6

 You'll always be the first and the last to wish me a Happy Birthday!!!

_____

_____

_____

_____

_____

_____

_____

_____

_____

_____

_____

_____

DAY 7

_You make me want to hold my breath in wonder to make each moment last just a little bit longer.

DAY 8

The moment you drunk from the milk carton
I knew...

DAY 9

_How does it feel to be the most beautiful woman in the room?

DAY 10

 Your regard for me gives me the fortitude to conquer any obstacle and the strength to overcome

_____

_____

_____

_____

_____

_____

_____

_____

_____

_____

_____

_____

DAY 11

Love **me** at my worst and know that I will be better for **you**.

_____

_____

_____

_____

_____

_____

_____

_____

_____

_____

_____

_____

DAY 12

The way you whisper until a scream is needed...

DAY 13

_You make me feel the music that before I just heard._____

_____

_____

_____

_____

_____

_____

_____

_____

_____

_____

_____

_____

DAY 14

Most of my questions are answered in your soul.

_____

_____

_____

_____

_____

_____

_____

_____

_____

_____

_____

_____

DAY 15

When we met, we knew...

_____

_____

_____

_____

_____

_____

_____

_____

_____

_____

_____

DAY 16

I want you to know that you've inspired me to do better.

DAY 17

 We're a team. God is our coach. The game plan is to work together and never give up on each other. 1, 2, 3 GO!

DAY 18

The very thought of you lives and breathes inside of me... This is how I go about searching for you.

_____

_____

_____

_____

_____

_____

_____

_____

_____

_____

_____

_____

DAY 19

_You're my metaphor for love and life._____

_____

_____

_____

_____

_____

_____

_____

_____

_____

_____

_____

_____

_____

DAY 20

I *ultimately* want what you can **ultimately** give.

DAY 21

I want to hide you in my wings and protect you from all of your biggest fears.

_____

_____

_____

_____

_____

_____

_____

_____

_____

_____

_____

DAY 22

This "JOY" I have in being in love with you...
That's where I AM!!!

_____

_____

_____

_____

_____

_____

_____

_____

_____

_____

_____

_____

DAY 23

I'll cosign all your eccentric thoughts.

_____

_____

_____

_____

_____

_____

_____

_____

_____

_____

_____

DAY 24

I can't wait to put a bow on you and place you under my tree.

DAY 25

_Gift me your trust and I'll spend my life thanking you.

DAY 26

I will gift you this... I'll leave nothing left unsaid.

DAY 27

FYI: You'll be married to me. *Not my family.*

_____

_____

_____

_____

_____

_____

_____

_____

_____

_____

_____

_____

_____

DAY 28

How about a 3 crossing wedding band?
Ecclesiastes 4:12 states "A cord of 3 is not
quickly broken" God. Husband and wife.

_____

_____

_____

_____

_____

_____

_____

_____

_____

_____

_____

_____

DAY 29

Thank you for not wanting to spend more time budgeting for the ceremony than you do wanting to make me a happy man. ☺

_____

_____

_____

_____

_____

_____

_____

_____

_____

_____

DAY 30

We met because we were meant to.

_____

_____

_____

_____

_____

_____

_____

_____

_____

_____

_____

_____

_____

DAY 31

I pray that my love notes & affirmations will have enough strength in their wings to find their way to you.

_____

_____

_____

_____

_____

_____

_____

_____

_____

_____

_____

NIGHT 31

<u>You and I were meant to be. Period. The End.</u> *Cue the happy ending music!*

.................................*10*.................................

.................................*9*.................................

.................................*8*.................................

.................................*7*.................................

.................................*6*.................................

.................................*5*.................................

.................................*4*.................................

.................................*3*.................................

.................................*2*.................................

.................................*1*.................................

...HAPPY......NEW......YEAR.....DARLING............

.................................Love Ramel.....

__P.S._____

____Will You Be My #Dear*Present*Wife?!?____

ABOUT THE AUTHOR

Truly to sing, takes a different breath and so it is this way with award winning singer, songwriter, educator, scholar, father and now author, Ramel Werner. Born in the *City of Wind*, Chicago, Illinois it is fitting that he shares every single breath he takes; deeply, effortlessly and positively on purpose in every note he sings and writes. Surrounded by dance-rhythms and the sound of music his entire life this soulful crooner grew up in a family where beats, verses and notes were a Rites of Passage into what would add to the many layers that compose who he is and has become.

With musicality literally and lyrically coursing through his veins; time and talent would formally usher Ramel to center stage for his initial solo performance, in the 8th grade. It was here where he first discovered his talent for songwriting, when he rewrote lyrics to the song "The Way We Were" by Barbara Streisand. Other stellar performances would follow at his high school and college alma maters Mendel Catholic in his hometown and Livingstone College located in Salisbury, North Carolina where this First Tenor/Baritone belted such classics as, "Two Occasions" written by Babyface Edmonds to standing ovation reception.

While majoring in Business Administration with a minor in Music, this melodist began to approach his relationship with word and sound differently. To the tuned epiphany that music is well said to be the speech of angels, he was destined to solidify his commitment and surrender to the power that music saves, delivers, heals and inspires. Embracing that music is the mediator between the spiritual and the sensual, this balladeer achieved musical success with his first independent project entitled, *Closure* in 2006. With such hits as "U Put It On Me," "Back In The Day," "Stay With Me," and "Rain," Ramel has led all who hears him to know and believe that music is the poetry of the air. Inspired by such gifted greats as Teddy Pendergrass, Luther Vandross and Eric Benet it is clear that his sonic path is grounded in soulful, heartfelt lyrical truth.

Winner of the 2010 British Academy of Golden Twits Award in Writing, 2011 in Music, and the 2012 Shorty Awards: Foursquare Mayor of the Year, this lyrical stylist holds a love for writing and has blogged

for http://byphaeth.wordpress.com/ and http://mylifekeys.com/. Additional musings can be read at

http://www.raelewisthornton.com/ and http://www.Designed2Prosper.blogspot.com. His forthcoming projects include a book series entitled, *Love Makes Sense* with his first installment being #DearFutureWife for obvious reasons. Realizing that life is a balanced system of learning and evolution, and the "purpose of it is to be useful," his dedication transcends beyond his uncompromising vocal ability to that of higher education and the classroom. Holding a Master's Degree in Behavior Disorders and Learning Disabilities from Dominican University, he received his Doctorate in Educational Leadership partnered with Harvard

University in July 2012. An educator of children challenged with disabilities for nearly two decades, Ramel seamlessly garners and holds the equilibrium of both worlds metronomically while learning from his students and being a conduit of positivity and change for those whose lives he has been entrusted to lead and guide daily.

Knowing that the pause is as important as the note, the wisdom of this lyrical craftsman overflows into his role of father to his daughter, Ryann. It is from this place first and foremost where the listener of this impassioned artist now author becomes convinced and committed to learning from him that music is what life sounds like, and writing is its validation.

More of Ramel's gifts can be found & followed here:

TWITTER : http://www.twitter.com/itsRamel
FACEBOOK: http://www.facebook.com/itsRamel
INSTAGRAM : itsRamel
SOUNDCLOUD : http://soundcloud.com/itsRamel
LINKEDIN : http://www.linkedin.com/in/ramel
WEBSITE : http://itsRamel.com/
GOOGLE + : Ramel Werner

www.ingramcontent.com/pod-product-compliance
Lightning Source LLC
LaVergne TN
LVHW051619080426
835511LV00016B/2078